What
Jesus
Did

31 devotions about the
life of Jesus

SINCLAIR B. FERGUSON

TRUTHFORLIFE®
CF4•K

10 9 8 7 6 5 4 3 2

Copyright © 2021 Sinclair B. Ferguson
Hardback ISBN: 978-1-5271-0799-1
Ebook ISBN: 978-1-5271-0856-1

Reprinted in 2022
by Christian Focus Publications,
Geanies House, Fearn, Tain, Ross-shire,
IV20 1TW, Scotland, U.K.
www.christianfocus.com
with
Truth For Life
P.O. Box 398000
Cleveland, Ohio 44139
truthforlife.org

Cover design and page layout by
James Amour
Printed and bound by Gutenberg, Malta

CONTENTS

Introduction

If you go to church or Sunday School, you have maybe heard grown-ups speaking about how important it is to spend time each day with the Lord Jesus, and to think about him.

I don't know about you, but I find it hard just to sit down and think. Sometimes my head feels empty. But then, at other times, it feels as though there are too many things to think about! So, it's not easy just to sit down and say to yourself, 'I am going to think about Jesus for the next five minutes.'

What helps me is when I have something to think about—something that makes me think! So, reading a book helps me. Or if someone asks a question. It's a bit like starting the engine in the car—something needs to turn the key or press the starter button. You read and then you start thinking. Or you hear the question and you try to work out the answer—so you start thinking! I have tried to put these two things together in this book. I hope that reading it will start you thinking about Jesus. In addition, since each of its chapters begins with a question, I hope that will help you think even more about him. Don't forget to ask for his help by using the prayers.

When I was at school we hardly ever spoke in class. We spent a lot of time writing. So I find writing helps me to think. Not everybody likes writing. But if you do, why don't you keep a little book and write down your thoughts about Jesus while you are reading this book? Who knows, maybe one day you'll write a book like this one!

But until you write your own book, I hope you will enjoy the one I have written for you!

Sinclair B. Ferguson

1. WHO NEEDED TO GET READY FOR CHRISTMAS?

Lord Jesus,
help me to think about you, learn
more about you, and love you today.

READ: JOHN 1:1-16

Do you look forward to Christmas every year?

We all try to get ready for Christmas, don't we? Mum has to get ready. She doesn't pull presents out of the sky already wrapped, does she?

A lot of people had to get ready for the first Christmas when Jesus was born. The Wise Men had to come from the East. Mary and Joseph had to come to Bethlehem. The shepherds weren't given any time at all to prepare, were they?

But who was first to start getting ready for that Christmas?

Was it Mary? She started getting ready about nine months before Jesus was born. That was when she heard he was coming. So she had a long time to get ready.

Or perhaps it was the angel, Gabriel, who told Mary she was going to have a baby?

Or maybe even the Wise Men, because they had to go on a long journey?

No. It was God. The Bible tells us that even before he had created the world, God the Father said to his Son, 'Once we've created this world something terrible is going to happen. Sin will spoil the world. Unless we decide to destroy the people we have made, we will need to do something to save them.'

The Lord Jesus said to his Heavenly Father, 'Father since that's going to happen, I'm willing to become a baby, grow up to be a man, and then die on the cross for the sins of the world.' And don't forget that God the Holy Spirit must have said, 'I'll be the one who will make it all happen.'

It's amazing that God the Father, the Son and the Holy Spirit prepared so long for Christmas.

Don't you think God must be very patient? He is patient with us. He is waiting for us to trust in the Lord Jesus as our Saviour. Don't let him wait any longer!

Heavenly Father,

Thank you that even before you made the world you knew that we would need a Saviour. Thank you, Lord Jesus, for coming to be the Saviour. And thank you, Holy Spirit, that you helped our Lord Jesus to be our Saviour.

Amen.

2. WHAT DID THE SHEPHERDS DO?

Lord Jesus,
help me to think about you, learn
more about you, and love you today.

READ: LUKE 2:1-20

Who, in the Christmas story, lived out in the fields near Bethlehem and heard about Jesus' birth in a spectacular way? Yes, the shepherds. The night Jesus was born a huge crowd of angels appeared. They were saying, 'Glory to God in the highest and on earth, peace.'

What do shepherds do? They look after people's sheep. Perhaps there were maybe five shepherds. I imagine they had quite a lot of sheep.

An angel told them, 'You've got to go to Bethlehem to see a new baby boy. He's the Saviour!'

What do you think the shepherds did? They said, 'Come on now, let's go.'

Have you ever wondered what happened to their sheep? Maybe one shepherd stayed to look after them. Or did the angels say they'd do that?

Sure enough, the shepherds found Jesus. He was in the stable part of a house in town. It must have been quite noisy—especially if the shepherds brought some of their sheep. Did Mary and Joseph ask them, 'What are you doing here? How did you know?'

On the way back to the fields, the shepherds told everybody who would listen all about what had happened.

I'm sure they never forgot that night.

How amazing it is that God brought all kinds of people (and perhaps some sheep as well!) to see the Lord Jesus. He will do that again, some day in the future. Our Lord Jesus will come back, and everything in the world, including sheep, will see Jesus and bow down before him, and call him Lord. Can you imagine what an amazing sight that will be? It will be worth waiting for!

We don't need to wait until that day to bow down to Jesus, do we? We can do that right now. Have you ever done that?

Heavenly Father,

We thank you that you sent your Son to be our Saviour, and one day he will return to this earth. Thank you that on that day the whole world will recognise him as Lord. But help us, we pray, to bow our hearts to him today, as well as on that day.

Amen.

3. WHO ARE THESE MEN ON CAMELS?

*Lord Jesus,
help me to think about you, learn
more about you, and love you today.*

READ: MATTHEW 2:1-8

How do Wise Men travel? The Wise Men who came to Bethlehem where Jesus was born had to make a long journey. They lived in the East, perhaps in Babylon. Babylon to Bethlehem is about 1,000 miles. They would have travelled by camels.

How many miles a day do you think a camel could travel with a Wise Man on its back? About twenty miles a day. At that rate it would have taken the Wise Men two months to get to Bethlehem.

Camels need lots of water. Did you know a camel can fill up its inner water tank with enough water for a week? A camel can drink twenty-five gallons of water in ten minutes!

But how did the Wise Men know where to go on their camels? God had made a star for them to follow. It seemed to tell them that a new King of the Jews was going to be born. They decided to go and worship him! However, near the end of their journey they thought, 'We should go to Jerusalem, the capital city, to find this new king.' That decision almost caused a disaster, but God saved them, and they eventually came to the house where the baby Jesus and his parents were staying.

The Wise Men had brought expensive gifts all that way for the new king. Do you know what the gifts were? They were: gold, frankincense, and myrrh.

Why do you think God wanted Wise Men from the East to come looking for the new King of the Jews? After all, they weren't Jews. He wasn't their king. Or was he?

Yes. Jesus wanted to be their king too. God had sent Jesus to be the Saviour of anyone in the whole wide world who would come to him and trust him.

You're in the wide world. Have you come to Jesus and trusted him as your Saviour?

Heavenly Father,

Thank you for the amazing way you touched the hearts of these Wise Men. They didn't have the Bible. They didn't fully understand what they were doing. Yet, you loved them, and you provided a star for them to follow. Lead us to Jesus too so that we may trust him as our Saviour, and worship him just like the Wise Men did.

Amen.

4. DO YOU NEED A COMPASS?

Lord Jesus,
help me to think about you, learn
more about you, and love you today.

READ: MATTHEW 2:9-12

Do you like to get presents at Christmas time? That's a silly question, isn't it? Have you ever had any unusual presents?

One Christmas I got three unusual presents: a calculator, some jokes, and a compass.

Would any of these have been useful for the Wise Men? Do you think they would have enjoyed telling each other jokes on their long journey? Or perhaps the calculator would have been useful for telling them how many miles they still had to go. Or do you think the most useful present would have been the compass? They didn't really need a compass, did they? God gave them a star to follow to Bethlehem.

But do you remember that they stopped in Jerusalem? They went to the King's Palace. The King's name was Herod. He was a horrible man. However, it was there that they were shown another compass. It turned out to be the best compass. And it is a compass that we need too. Can you guess what that compass was?

When Herod heard that the Wise Men had come to worship the new king, he asked the people who knew their Bible best, 'Where is this king going to be born?' They said, 'The Bible points to Bethlehem as the place of his birth.'

Herod didn't want to worship any new king! But the Wise Men set off. God's Word told them how to find Jesus. That's what it's for. It's our compass!

Did you know there's something amazing about the needle in a compass? It always points in the same direction – to the north. God's compass, the Bible, always points in the same direction too, doesn't it? It always points to Jesus, so that we can learn about him, trust him, and love him.

Has the Bible pointed you to Jesus?

Lord Jesus,

We thank you for giving us a compass in the Bible. Thank you for the way it tells us all about you. Thank you for all you have done for us. And thank you that you are still called 'Jesus' so we can still trust you as our Saviour. We want to do that with all our hearts.

Amen.

5. WHAT DO YOU KNOW ABOUT JESUS AND HIS MOTHER?

*Lord Jesus,
help me to think about you, learn
more about you, and love you today.*

READ: LUKE 2:25-35

Where was Jesus before he was born? He was inside his mum. He wasn't able to speak. He couldn't use a knife and fork. He needed his mum to survive in there—just as we did once too! Of course, his Heavenly Father was watching over him. There were also angels watching over him. And the Holy Spirit was watching over him too.

For several months Jesus was inside his mother Mary. Whatever she was eating and drinking was feeding him too! Mums are special because through them God has given us our lives!

When Jesus was dying, the very last thing he told his mum was that his friend, John, would look after her. He loved his mum very much.

When we love Jesus, we begin to love our mums more too. My mum is no longer alive, but I wish I could go to her and say, 'Thank you for looking after me even before I was born.'

Soon after Jesus was born, Mary and Joseph took him to the temple in Jerusalem. An old man called Simeon told Mary, 'A sword will pierce through your own soul.' I wonder if she remembered those words as she later watched Jesus dying. She must have been very sore.

Mary knew Jesus was to be the Saviour. But sometimes she found it difficult to understand exactly how God was going to make that happen. She worried about him—just like your mum sometimes worries about you. And she had a big family to look after as well. We know Jesus had four brothers and probably at least three sisters! And they all worried about him because at first they didn't understand that he had come into the world to die for our sins.

However, isn't it wonderful that Jesus' own family came to trust in him as their Saviour and Lord?

And Jesus didn't come only for his own family. He loves our families too. That's why we can trust him. He loves us just as much as he loved Mary and Joseph and his brothers and sisters.

Do you ever think about that?

Lord Jesus,

Thank you that you loved your family so much and cared for your mother Mary. We pray that you would help us all to trust and love you. And help us to love everyone in our family as well. Be with us we pray.

Amen.

Lord Jesus,
help me to think about you, learn
more about you, and love you today.

READ: HEBREWS 2:14-18

Do you know the Christmas Carol 'Away in a Manger'? One of its verses begins,

> *The cattle are lowing, the baby awakes,*
> *But little Lord Jesus, no crying he makes*

Do you think the baby Jesus never cried? All babies cry, don't they? So, it is certain that the baby Jesus cried. After all, that's what you do when you're a baby. If you are uncomfortable, or sore, or hungry, it's the only way you can tell everyone you need help.

It's amazing that God's Son came into the world and shared all our experiences. He was once a baby boy! He created the whole world. But when he came into the world, there must have been times when he was uncomfortable or hungry and cried.

But perhaps the person who wrote the hymn was thinking about a night when one of the cows woke Jesus up and he just lay there listening to it moo?

The baby Jesus definitely cried though. One of the other Christmas hymns says, *Tears and smiles like us he knew.*

But why did God's Son become a baby? Because he wanted to be our Saviour and Friend right from the very beginning of life. If he had come into the world as a grown man, he would never have known what it is like to be seven years old, or ten, or twelve. But now we know that he understands us even when we are children.

So we don't need to wait until we are grown up to tell him that we want to trust and love him. When we do trust and love him, we will discover that he is a wonderful Saviour and the Best Friend we could possibly have.

Lord Jesus,

Thank you that when you came into the world you came as a little baby. You knew what it was to be uncomfortable, and to cry because you didn't know any words to speak. And as you grew older you were sometimes lonely and sad. Thank you that there is nothing that you do not know. We trust you and we love you. Please bless our family.

Amen.

7. WHO KNEW FIRST?

*Lord Jesus,
help me to think about you, learn
more about you, and love you today.*

READ: LUKE 1:26-38

Do you know who was the first to hear that Jesus was going to be born?

Was it the shepherds? Well, no; they didn't hear until after Jesus had been born.

Was it the Wise Men? They had a long, long journey to go. No, I don't think it was them. They wouldn't have taken nine months to get to Bethlehem.

Then it must have been Mary! She had known for nine months. But no, it wasn't Mary.

So, if it wasn't the Wise Men, or the shepherds, or Mary, who did God tell first?

Well, who told Mary? It was the angel Gabriel.

Do you know what the name Gabriel means? It means, 'God is mighty'. I wonder if, when God was deciding which angel he would send, he thought, 'Since my Son is the mighty God, I think I'll send the angel whose name means "God is mighty".'

So Gabriel could have said, 'I was the first one to hear.' But it doesn't matter all that much who was the first to hear the news, does it? The important thing was that everybody heard it—Mary and Joseph, the Shepherds, the Wise Men, and everyone with whom they shared the news.

If you read Matthew's Gospel you will see something very interesting. It begins with people coming from far away to learn about Jesus. It ends with Jesus telling his disciples to go to people far away, everywhere in the world, to tell them the good news about his love.

It's still important that everybody hears about Jesus. Perhaps you are the only one of your friends who has heard the good news about Jesus. Do you think you could tell them about him? We can ask him to help us to do that. And when we do, we'll be like the angel Gabriel! Isn't that amazing?

Lord Jesus,

We thank you that your Father sent the angel, Gabriel, to tell Mary you were going to be born. Thank you for the way the news spread. We know that it hasn't reached some people yet. Please send Christians to tell them. And please help us to tell someone else about you.

Amen.

Lord Jesus,
help me to think about you, learn
more about you, and love you today.

READ: GENESIS 3:1-15

Have you ever wished that Christmas Day would last longer? I used to try wrapping up my presents again and then opening them the next day. But I still couldn't make Christmas last!

Is there any way we can make Christmas last? Perhaps. But first, we need to go right back to the very beginning. The apostle John, who loved Jesus so much, wrote this in one of his letters: 'For this purpose the Son of God was manifested, that He might destroy the works of the devil' (you'll find the words in 1 John 3:8).

What did he mean? Do you remember what happened in the Garden of Eden? The devil came to Adam and Eve through a serpent. He told them a lie about God, and they listened to him instead of to their loving Father! Everything went wrong after that. Jesus came into the world to put things right again.

To bring us back to our Heavenly Father, and to make things right and new again, Jesus first had to tear down what the devil had done.

Long ago, God promised Adam and Eve that someone in their family tree would defeat the devil! But that person would be harmed in the process. That promise can be found in Genesis 3:15. It is the oldest promise of salvation. It was the very first promise God ever gave that Jesus would come to be the Saviour we all need. It was also the hardest promise to keep that God has ever made. It meant that Jesus would have to die on the cross for us.

God kept that promise. Jesus kept it! On the cross Jesus conquered the devil. He took away our sins. When we trust in him, we are forgiven forever. Jesus has the power to destroy all the devil's work. The devil took us away from God, but Jesus can make things right again and help us to live for our loving Father.

The only way we can make Christmas last is to have Jesus as our Saviour and Friend.

Lord Jesus,

Thank you for coming into the world to be our Saviour. Because you are our Saviour, we know that the real joy of Christmas can last all year long. We know that you will be with us and we can have you as our Saviour and Friend forever. Thank you so much.

Amen.

9. WHY DID JESUS BECOME A REFUGEE?

Lord Jesus,
help me to think about you, learn
more about you, and love you today.

READ: MATTHEW 2:13-23

What is the very first thing that you can remember? The first thing I remember in my whole life is standing up in my cot and crying! I was thinking, 'Let me out of here!'

What is your very first memory?

Here's another question: What do you think Jesus' first memory was? If he didn't remember it, I am sure Mary told him later about the night she woke him up and they left Bethlehem and began the long journey to Egypt. Jesus would have been too young to understand what Joseph had said to Mary: 'We've got to leave Bethlehem, Mary. King Herod is going to try to kill Jesus!' Horrid, wicked Herod. So, Mary and Joseph bundled up Jesus that night and fled to Egypt.

I wonder if they kept looking behind to see if anyone was chasing them.

What do we call someone who has to leave their home and go to another country for safety? Yes, 'a refugee'.

Why would God the Father let that happen to his Son, Jesus? It must have been a ghastly journey. And perhaps when they got to Egypt at first Mary and Joseph didn't understand the accent very well. Everything would have been a bit different. Maybe they had relatives there. But maybe they didn't know anybody. That would have been difficult. Just as well the Wise men had brought them some gold. That would help them rent a house and buy what they needed. However, they must have felt they didn't really belong there. Have you ever felt that?

So, why did God allow this to happen? Here is one important answer:

God allowed this to happen to the Lord Jesus so that no boy or girl could ever have such a difficult experience and say, 'Lord Jesus, you don't understand.' Because he does understand. Jesus understands everything we go through. He has been through worse.

Will you remember that, if things get difficult, Jesus understands? He wants to help you.

Lord Jesus,

Help us when we face difficulties. Help us to understand that you use all these things to bring us closer to you. Thank you for all the ways you have been with us already. Please continue to help and bless us.

Amen.

Lord Jesus,
help me to think about you, learn
more about you, and love you today.

READ: MATTHEW 11:28-30

If Jesus walked into the room, would you know who he was?

Can you recognise someone when you can't see them? Yes, you can. Isn't it amazing that you can recognise people just by hearing their voice?

But how would you recognise Jesus when you haven't actually heard him speak? When he was on earth, he didn't speak English – he spoke Aramaic and perhaps sometimes Greek.

So how can you recognise Jesus?

Was there something special about him? There were lots of special things about him. When children met

Jesus, they felt there was something wonderful about him that they didn't feel about other people. He was special.

Jesus is still that way. The Letter to the Hebrews 13:8, tells us that 'Jesus Christ is the same yesterday and today and forever.' Every time you read about him in the Gospels you should try to remember this: he is the same Jesus today as he was then!

One wonderful thing about Jesus is that even if you tell him the worst things about yourself, he will still love you. And he will forgive you, and help you to be more like him, if you ask him. That's something that makes him different.

You wouldn't want to tell me all the bad things you've done, would you? But with Jesus, once you start telling him about yourself you will want to tell him absolutely everything, even the bad things. He will listen to you and forgive you if you ask him.

When that happens, it is like being wrapped in his big arms and hearing him say, 'That's not a surprise to me. I knew all about you and I was just waiting for you to tell me everything about yourself. I have been wanting to forgive you!'

That's one of the most wonderful things about the Lord Jesus.

Lord Jesus,

You know everything about us and there is nothing in our lives that takes you by surprise. You know the good things and the bad things, the sad things, and the happy things. We trust you and we love you too, and we want you to be with us forever.

Amen.

11. IS JESUS WATCHING?

*Lord Jesus,
help me to think about you, learn
more about you, and love you today.*

READ: LUKE 22:32-34

Do you know anything about Simon Peter? He was one of Jesus' friends. In fact he was one of his very best friends, wasn't he?

But sometimes Peter didn't behave like a best friend. The night before the Lord Jesus was crucified, Peter was asked if he knew him. Can you believe what he did? It was the very worst thing he had ever done in his life. He said, 'I don't know Jesus at all.' Three times this happened.

Then, when he looked up, he saw Jesus standing there, watching him!

Peter ran away and cried and cried. I don't think he felt that Jesus was angry with him. He had probably seen a look of sadness in Jesus' eyes. He saw how much Jesus loved him. But he had let Jesus down.

Peter was so sorry. He cried and cried. What made it worse was that he saw in Jesus' eyes how much he loved him. If only he could know that Jesus would forgive him!

Did Jesus forgive him? Yes, Jesus prayed for Peter and forgave him. He loved him enough to die for him on the cross.

We have all let Jesus down, haven't we? Sometimes we don't let people know we follow the Lord Jesus because like Peter we are a bit frightened of what they will say or do. Do you ever wonder if Jesus can forgive you? Jesus forgave Peter. Three times Peter denied Jesus. Later on Jesus asked Peter three times, 'Peter, do you love me?' When he said 'Yes, Lord', Jesus told him that in the future he would have the courage even to die for him!

Jesus can forgive you too. He watches us and loves us. If we fail him, he wants us to ask for his forgiveness and help. Let's always do that. You can do it now.

Lord Jesus,

We thank you that you see us, even when we forget you. Sometimes we do things that we know displease you. We're so sorry. Thank you that you don't stop loving us. Thank you for dying for our sins. We're really sorry for them. Please forgive us.

Amen.

Lord Jesus,
help me to think about you, learn
more about you, and love you today.

READ: LUKE 22:54–62

Did you know that the Bible says the devil is like a lion? Peter wrote: 'The devil walks about like a roaring lion, seeking whom he may devour' (1 Peter 5:8).

Peter had experienced that himself. Remember what happened the night Jesus was captured? Peter followed him to the High Priest's house. He got as near as possible. It was cold, and he was trying to get warm at a fire when a servant girl asked him, 'Do you know Jesus?'

Peter was frightened and said, very quickly, 'No, I don't know him; 'Oh', she said, 'Are you telling the truth? Don't you know Jesus?' 'No, no!' Peter said. 'Oh', the little girl said, 'you look like one of his disciples.' Peter said. 'Never, never, never.' And he moved away. But then another girl came up and asked him the same question. And then some of the men who were there came over to him and said, 'You sound as though you come from near Jesus' home in Galilee. You must know him! Tell us the truth.' Peter went into a panic. 'No, I don't know the man!' He even started swearing as though he couldn't possibly be a disciple of Jesus.

The devil, like a roaring lion, had caught him. He felt he was being eaten up by him. He remembered that Jesus had warned him the devil wanted to do that to him. It was awful.

Then he remembered something else Jesus had said: 'I have prayed for you Peter that you don't lose your faith. I will hold on to you.' He began to cry. His tears were a mixture of sorrow and relief. He had sinned; but Jesus still loved him. He was like a little lamb that had been caught by a roaring lion; but Jesus, his Good Shepherd, had promised to rescue him.

Later, when Peter was writing to his Christian friends, he taught them how the devil is like a lion. They all knew his story, and all about how Jesus had rescued him.

That is important to remember, isn't it? The devil tries to tear us away from loving Jesus. But Jesus has promised never, ever, ever to let us go.

Lord Jesus,

Thank you that you are the Good Shepherd who can rescue us from the devil when he roars like a lion and tries to destroy our faith. Help us to be strong. Protect us when we are tempted. Rescue us if we fail. Thank you that you will never leave us.

Amen.

13. WOULD YOU LIKE TO SPEND A WEEK WITH JESUS?

*Lord Jesus,
help me to think about you, learn
more about you, and love you today.*

READ: ACTS 1:1-5

Do you know what a Gospel is? The first four books of the New Testament are called 'Gospels'. That means good news. They tell us the good news about the Lord Jesus. That's why we love to read them!

The fourth Gospel was written by John. Near the beginning of his story, he tells us about the first week Jesus' disciples spent with him. And then at the end he does it again, but this time tells us about their last week with him before he died.

What do you think it would be like to be with Jesus for a whole week? Imagine waking up one morning and discovering that he was standing at your bedside saying, 'Come on! Wake up! I am going to spend this week with you. And you are going to spend this week with me!'

Would that week be just the same as any other week? Or would it be different? Don't you think it would be amazing to go through a whole week knowing that Jesus would be with you?

But the Lord Jesus has promised to be with us every day, every week, hasn't he? So, if that's true, we need to remember that he is with us. When you are a Christian the Lord Jesus walks beside you every moment of the day. He has promised he will never leave us!

Being a Christian means trusting the Lord Jesus and living in his presence. You can tell him about everything. You can tell him what you are enjoying. And you can tell him when things are difficult, 'Lord Jesus help me here.' You can even tell him, 'Lord Jesus I really messed up there. Forgive me.'

Every day, when you wake up in the morning, try to think about this: The Lord Jesus has promised to be with me every week, every day, every hour and every minute!

The Bible tells us that although we can't see Jesus, he is with us. We love him because he first loved us.

Lord Jesus,

Thank you that you are with us. Help us to pray for each other, and for people who are sad or ill. We know that you are with us this week. You've promised! Help us to live in your presence.

Amen.

Lord Jesus,
help me to think about you, learn
more about you, and love you today.

READ: PSALM 96:1-13

Do you enjoy going to church and singing to God?

Here is a more important question: Do you think God enjoys being with us at church when we sing to him?

How do we know if God enjoys being at church? Anyway, what does he do when he comes?

Here are three verses from the Bible that tell us what God enjoys. One verse is about God the Father, another about God the Son, our Lord Jesus, and the third is about the Holy Spirit.

God the Father enjoys singing.
Zephaniah 3:17 says, 'The LORD your God in your midst ... he will rejoice over you with gladness ... he

will rejoice over you with singing.' If you enjoy a song on the radio, or on a speaker, what do you sometimes do? You sing along, don't you? When we sing about how much we love Jesus, God the Father sings along! He loves to hear us singing about the Lord Jesus, his Son.

God the Son enjoys leading our worship.
Hebrews 2:12 tells us that the Lord Jesus says, 'I will declare Your name to My brethren; in the midst of the assembly I will sing praise to You.' Did you know Jesus does that? Right in the middle of the congregation, when we are praising God together, Jesus is there leading our singing! He is saying to us, 'Come on now, let's praise God the Father together.'

God the Holy Spirit enjoys helping us to worship.
Paul says in Ephesians 5:18-19, 'Be filled with the Spirit, speaking to one another in psalms and hymns and spiritual songs, singing and making melody in your heart to the Lord.' The Holy Spirit always loves to help us praise the Father and the Son.

Will you remember that the next time you are in church? It's amazing, isn't it?

Heavenly Father, Lord Jesus Christ, Wonderful Holy Spirit,

Thank you that you not only receive our worship, but you love being with us, and you love helping us to worship and praise you. Help us to remember this and to worship you with all our hearts.

Amen.

15. WHAT WOULD YOU DO IF YOU KNEW JESUS WAS COMING?

*Lord Jesus,
help me to think about you, learn
more about you, and love you today.*

READ: ACTS 1:6-11

Would you get excited if you knew someone important was coming to see you? You would try to get ready for them, wouldn't you?

What would you do if someone like a King or a Queen or a President was planning to come to dinner at your house? Would your mother start planning a special meal? Would you help to clean the house from top to bottom? Would you make sure your room was tidy? Or would you say, 'That's nothing special!' I don't think so!

Now, imagine The Most Powerful Person in the World was coming. Would you get ready?

Who is The Most Powerful person in the World? It's Jesus, of course. He said, 'All authority in heaven and on earth has been given to me.' And he is coming! In fact, he wants to come to be with us every single day! We don't see him; but we know he is with us.

However, Jesus also promised that one day, sometime in the future, he will come so that everyone will see him. Everyone will bow down before him. On that day Jesus will show how powerful he is by making everything right again and making it new. In fact, on that day, wherever you look, everything you see will shine with his glory. What a sight that will be!

Are you ready for Jesus to come to be with you? And are you ready for the day when everyone will see him? When you don't know exactly when someone is coming you try to be ready every day! It's wonderful to be ready for the coming of the Lord Jesus every single day. He reminds us of that every Sunday when we go to church. He promised that even if we are in a tiny congregation he will come: 'For where two or three are gathered in My name, I am there in the midst of them' (Matthew 18:20).

And then, at the end of time, he will come and everyone will see him. What a great day that will be! So, let's be ready for Jesus to come!

Lord Jesus,

Thank you that you come to us. Help us to look forward to being with you. Help us to look forward to your final coming. Thank you that in the meantime you will never leave us and that you will always take care of us.

Amen.

16. CAN ANYONE SNEAK UP ON JESUS?

Lord Jesus,
help me to think about you, learn
more about you, and love you today.

READ: MARK 5:21-43

Did people ever try to sneak up on Jesus so that nobody would see them?

Nicodemus tried. You can read about him in John's Gospel chapter 3. He was a famous Jewish teacher. He tried to sneak up on Jesus so that nobody would know he was visiting him. So, he came to see Jesus at night. Later on, John tells us that, when Jesus died, Nicodemus came out into the open. He helped his friend Joseph of Arimathea lovingly put Jesus' body in a tomb Joseph owned.

On another occasion, a lady who had been ill for twelve years planned to sneak up on Jesus without anybody knowing what she was going to do. None of her doctors had helped her, but she heard that Jesus could heal people. So, she thought, 'If I can just sneak up and touch Jesus, even touch his clothes, I might be healed.'

She pressed through the crowd and got in just beside Jesus, reached out her hand, and touched his robe. She had done it! And she was immediately healed!

But then Jesus stopped and said, 'Who touched me?' He had felt healing power leave him. The woman knew that she had to step forward and admit she had touched him.

She was shaking. No wonder. I would be shaking too! Do you think she maybe thought that Jesus was going to give her a telling-off in front of everybody?

No! Jesus was far too kind to do that! He wanted to explain to her why she had been healed. It was not because she had touched him, but because she had trusted him. He wanted her to know that she could trust him for absolutely everything.

You don't need to sneak up on Jesus. He already knows all about you! You can bring all your troubles to him, and tell him all about yourself. And here's the best thing. He knows all about you. And he is very, very kind.

Lord Jesus,

You know everything about us. You know more about us than even our mums and dads do! We thank you that you keep loving us. Help us to keep loving you too. Please strengthen us to be your witnesses.

Amen.

17. CAN JESUS HELP US TO DO WHAT WE CAN'T DO?

Lord Jesus,
help me to think about you, learn
more about you, and love you today.

READ: MATTHEW 14:13-21

Would the Lord Jesus ever ask you to do something you couldn't do?

One day Jesus went for a long walk with his disciples into the hills. As he was sitting down he noticed a crowd of people coming towards them. It was huge—even just counting the men he could see there must be about five thousand! They had come a distance, and Jesus thought to himself, 'They've come all this way; they'll be hungry.' So, he asked Philip, one of the disciples, 'Where can we get food for these people?'

Philip thought, 'We're miles from any shops; surely he knows the answer is obvious: nowhere!' He said, 'Jesus, even if I had saved up last year's wages it wouldn't be enough to buy food for this crowd. It's huge!'

Now here is something very interesting: John tells us Jesus was just testing Philip! He knew all the time what he was going to do! But what was that?

Peter's brother Andrew found a boy who was willing to share his lunch with Jesus!

Jesus took the boy's bread rolls and fish and prayed that God would bless them. He started giving the food to his disciples and told them to share it round the crowd. And as they did—amazingly—it fed all the people and there were leftovers!

Two things had happened. Jesus did something miraculous—he fed the huge crowd. But there was something else. Jesus made it possible for the disciples to do things they knew they couldn't do. And he used the young boy's gift in a way he could never have imagined.

That's the kind of thing Jesus does! There are lessons for us here, aren't there? When we give what we have to Jesus, he uses it. And when we know there are things that need to be done but we can't do them, Jesus will help us. The apostle Paul discovered this. He wrote, 'I can do all things through Christ who strengthens me' (Philippians 4:13). What a great Saviour and Friend Jesus is!

Lord Jesus,

Thank you for your wonderful love for us. Thank you that you use everything we give to you, and you help us to do things that we're not strong or wise enough to do ourselves. Please help us to love you and to trust you with everything we have.

Amen.

Lord Jesus,
help me to think about you, learn
more about you, and love you today.

READ: 1 CORINTHIANS 15:1-11

Did you know that Jesus knew he was going to die in Jerusalem?

Jesus' disciples had been with him for a couple of years. They thought they knew him really well. But then he began to teach them that he would be captured, beaten and killed.

How was Jesus killed? He died on a cross. He was nailed to a wooden bar on a tree trunk and left to die. We call that 'crucifixion'. It is a terrible way to die, isn't it?

But why did Jesus have to die on a cross?

In the Old Testament there is a verse that says 'a hanged man is cursed by God'. You can find it in Deuteronomy 21:23. When Jesus was crucified, he was hanged on a tree.

Now, here is something we must never, ever forget. Jesus' Heavenly Father arranged this. And his Son, the Lord Jesus agreed to come into the world to die. He was hanged on a tree and became a curse.

Did Jesus deserve that? No, he didn't. But it was all part of God's plan to save us from our sin. God the Father knew we could never pay the penalty for our own sins. He sent his Son, the Lord Jesus, and he came willingly to do that. The Holy Spirit promised to support and strengthen him for his task.

On the cross, Jesus experienced what our sins deserve; he even felt forsaken by God! But he trusted him; and the Holy Spirit helped him. This was all God's own amazing idea. And he had it because he loved us so much.

We are the ones who have sinned, not Jesus. But Jesus died on the cross, so that we don't need to die for our sins. So now we can say to him, 'Lord Jesus, thank you that you did this for me'.

That's why Jesus died on the cross.

Lord Jesus,

It's terrible to think that you died on a cross. Our sins must be awful if you needed to do that. We can never thank you enough that, helped by the Holy Spirit, you came to take our place and bear our sins. Thank you that now we can live forever in your presence. We love you so much. Be with us today.

Amen.

19. WHAT WOULD CSI JERUSALEM HAVE FOUND?

*Lord Jesus,
help me to think about you, learn
more about you, and love you today.*

READ: MATTHEW 28:1-15

Do you watch TV? I like crime programmes on TV! Some of the programmes I watch are about CSI teams. CSI stands for Crime Scene Investigation.

Members of CSI teams look for clues. If the criminals are not wearing gloves, their fingers leave marks—fingerprints—on the things they touched. Everybody's fingerprints are different. So, if there are fingerprints you can find out whose they are! Clues are very important.

Would a CSI team have found any clues if they had investigated Jesus' resurrection?

Soldiers had been positioned to guard Jesus' tomb. But they couldn't stop Jesus coming back to life and walking out of the tomb! The religious leaders who had wanted Jesus to be crucified told them, 'We will give you money if you will say that Jesus' disciples came and stole his body away.' So, the soldiers took the money, and started telling lies.

If the CSI team had gone to the tomb, would they have found that it was empty? That's a trick question. Jesus was no longer there; but the tomb wasn't empty! He had left something behind. He had taken off the covering on his body and folded it up. He even folded up the cloth that had been placed over his face. He deliberately left clues! It was as if he had borrowed the tomb and the grave clothes, but left them behind because he didn't need them any longer!

All this was evidence that Jesus' body had not been stolen. If you were a body thief you wouldn't take off those clothes, and fold them up neatly! No, you'd get out of the tomb as quickly as you could—especially knowing there were soldiers around!

Jesus' body was not stolen. He had risen from the dead, taken off the clothes in which he had been buried, folded them up, put the face cloth in a separate place, and walked out of the tomb!

Jesus left clues behind so that the disciples would know he was alive, even before they saw him again. And now he is alive for evermore.

Lord Jesus,

You died for our sins and came back to life to be our Saviour and our Lord. Be with us and help us, we pray, throughout all our life. We praise and thank you for all you have done for us, and we trust you as our Saviour and Lord.

Amen.

20. CAN YOU GET OUT OF THE DEBTORS' PRISON?

Lord Jesus,
help me to think about you, learn
more about you, and love you today.

READ: MATTHEW 6:7–15

Do you know what it means to be in debt? It means you owe somebody and have to pay them back. Maybe one day you will read a famous book called *Little Dorrit*, or perhaps watch the movie. Little Dorrit's father was in the Debtors' Prison in London. But if you are in the Debtors' Prison, you can't earn the money you need to pay your debts.

Are you in debt to anyone? Think what it would feel like if you owed money to your mum or dad for all the clothes you have worn, all the meals you have eaten, all the holidays you have been on and everything else you've had! Can you afford to pay them back?

So, why are you not in the Debtors' Prison? Because mum and dad have paid it all themselves!

We are all in debt to God, aren't we? Everything we have we owe to him. We can never pay him back. But he has told us we don't need to. He has provided it all for us.

But there are other debts we owe him. When we pray the Lord's Prayer we say, 'forgive us our debts'. Those debts are not the gifts God has given us but the sins we have committed.

We owe it to God our Father to love and obey him. But, instead, we commit sins. These are debts to him we cannot repay even if we try. Every day it is like being in the Debtors' Prison in London: our debt gets bigger and bigger. And we still cannot pay it. If only somebody could pay our debts for us!

Somebody has. God's Son, the Lord Jesus, came into the world and obeyed God in our place. And then he died on the cross to pay all of our debts. When we trust in him, they are all forgiven—every single one of them! Isn't that great?

Sometimes people who know they have sinned try to pay back the debt they owe to God. But they can't. Only Jesus can; and he has. That's why we call him Saviour.

Have you ever asked God to forgive your debts?

Lord Jesus,

Thank you for all the wonderful things you have done for us. Today we specially thank you for paying our debts. We pray that the burden of them all will be lifted off us. Help us to follow you happily all our lives.

Amen.

21. DID JESUS LEAVE ANYTHING FOR SUPPER?

Lord Jesus,
help me to think about you, learn
more about you, and love you today.

READ: MATTHEW 26:17-30

Do you ever get visitors to your house? Maybe some of them make you feel, 'I wish you would leave!' But if someone makes you feel happy, when they leave you feel a bit sad, don't you?

A few weeks after his resurrection Jesus went back to heaven. The disciples must have wanted him to stay, don't you think? How often they had enjoyed having a meal with him and sitting round a table listening to what he had to say.

It must have been wonderful to sit at a table with Jesus; but now he was leaving them. When would they see him again?

We don't know when we will see Jesus. We must wait. Our Saviour knew that wouldn't be easy. So, while he was having his last meal with his disciples, just before he was captured, he did something wonderful. He gave them a kind of miniature meal. He broke off some bread and passed it round for each of the disciples to take a piece and eat it. And he passed round a cup of wine and told them all to drink from it. He gave them the bread and the wine as pictures of the sacrifice of his body and blood on the Cross.

We still do that in church. Everyone who trusts in the Lord Jesus is given a piece of bread to eat and a little wine to drink. It's very simple. We can't see Jesus; but the bread and the wine are his little gifts to us. Through them he is saying, 'See how much I love you, and remember I am with you, and I have promised to come back again.'

We call this 'The Lord's Supper'. Jesus invites his children to come into his presence, and to sit at the table with him. So, what they see with their eyes, and touch with their hands, and taste on their tongues, they also do in their hearts, thanking Jesus for his love. One day Jesus will come again. Until then he gives his children this little meal to keep them going! He thinks of everything!

Lord Jesus,

Thank you for showing us your love in the broken bread and the poured-out wine. Thank you that every time we see them, we remember all you did for us. And thank you too that the Lord's Supper makes the church long even more to see you face to face.

Amen.

Lord Jesus,
help me to think about you, learn
more about you, and love you today.

READ: MATTHEW 19:13-15

Do you think Jesus loves children? After all, there are some grown-ups who don't!

Maybe some of Jesus' disciples were like that. When some mums and dads brought their boys and girls and even their babies to the Lord Jesus for his blessing, these disciples said, 'Shhhh. Shhhh! Out of the way! Jesus can't see you today'.

Do you know what Jesus did? He said to the disciples, 'Don't do that again. I love children. Let them come to me!' So the children came. Perhaps some of them ran to him. But others were so small their mums and dads had to carry them. And Jesus picked them up, put his hands on them, and gave them God's blessing. And we know that when Jesus blesses people they really are blessed! Imagine being able to say, 'The Lord Jesus blessed me!'

You might think, 'That was all very well for them. But how can we know Jesus loves us and blesses us?'

There are lots of reasons we know that Jesus loves us. But the most important one is that he died on the cross to take away our sins, so that we could be with him forever. Jesus wants us to live with him forever because he loves us so much. He wants us to enjoy being with him.

Here is a verse from a hymn that tells us about Jesus' love:

> *Jesus loves me! he who died*
> *Heaven's gate to open wide;*
> *He will wash away my sin,*
> *Let his little child come in.*
> *Yes! Jesus loves me!*
> *The Bible tells me so.*

That's really true!

Lord Jesus,

Thank you so much for loving us. Thank you that you have proved you love us so much by dying for us on the cross. We praise you for this. And we thank you for your promise to be with us forever. Help us to love you too, and to enjoy being your disciples.

Amen.

23. WHAT CAN I GIVE TO JESUS?

Lord Jesus,
help me to think about you, learn
more about you, and love you today.

READ: MARK 12:41-44

Do you ever go shopping?

Sometimes I go to the supermarket. I like to hand over real money rather than use a credit card. Sometimes, when I have been in the United States of America, I have noticed that if I hand over a twenty-dollar bill, the person at the check-out will run something that looks like a pen over it to make sure it's real. Maybe I have a dishonest face!

What if Jesus checks up to see if we are real—and mean what we say?

Perhaps you sing songs in your church about how much you love Jesus, and that you want to give everything to him. Jesus can tell if we really mean it, can't he? He doesn't need a special pen. He sees into our hearts.

One day when Jesus was in the temple in Jerusalem, he saw a lady who was a widow (that's a woman whose husband has died). He watched her putting two small coins into the offering box. Maybe he heard them hit the bottom. He could tell she hadn't put in much money. But somehow Jesus knew it was all she had. Do you know what he said? I wonder if she heard him. He said that what she gave was worth more than the money all the rich people had put in.

But how could that be? Jesus said it was because she gave God everything she had. Perhaps God kept his eye on her two coins and somehow used them in wonderful ways, while he didn't do anything special with the rich people's gifts. If Jesus could feed thousands of people from a few rolls and a couple of fish, God must have ways of using small coins.

So, whether we are young and feel we don't have much to give to the Lord Jesus, or get old and still feel we don't have much to give to him, let's give everything we have to him. For when we love him with all our heart, God will bless and use our gifts.

So, don't hold back anything from Jesus.

Lord Jesus,

Thank you that you can do big things even with the little we can give to you. We want to give our lives to you. Please do whatever you want with them. We do love you and we pray that you would help us to believe that you can use us for your glory.

Amen.

24. DO YOU HAVE A NICKNAME?

Lord Jesus,
help me to think about you, learn
more about you, and love you today.

READ: JOHN 13:1-17

Do you know what a nickname is? It's a name your friends give to you that's different from the one your mum and dad gave you!

Some of Jesus' disciples had nicknames. James and John, who were brothers, were called 'Sons of Thunder'. What do you think that said about them? There were two disciples called Judas; one was probably known as Thaddaeus. The other was called Judas Iscariot. Maybe 'Iscariot' was a nickname.

'Iscariot' could mean 'the man from Kerioth'. Or it could mean 'bag man' since Judas was the person who kept the disciples' money in a bag—and stole from it.

Or maybe it meant 'knife man'. That's a bit scary, isn't it? Judas was the disciple who betrayed Jesus.

Jesus knew that Judas would do that. Yet just before Judas betrayed him, Jesus knelt down in front of him to wash his dirty feet. Imagine it! You would think that when Jesus shows kindness and love to people they would love him back. But people are not always like that with Jesus.

Sometimes they're not like that with us. They turn against us because we love and serve Jesus.

There's something else we learn from Judas, isn't there? It's this: watching Jesus, and listening to his teaching, even being with people who trust and love Jesus, isn't the same as trusting and loving him for yourself.

Judas turned his back on Jesus.

Simon Peter also turned his back on Jesus and denied him. So, what was the difference? Peter wept because he had let Jesus down, and Jesus forgave him. Judas regretted what he had done. But he never seems to have asked to be forgiven.

Remember that if you let the Lord Jesus down. Don't be like Judas. Remember Peter. Tell the Lord Jesus you are sorry, and come back to him.

Lord Jesus,

We often let you down and we want to tell you how sorry we are. Please always take us back. We thank you that the Bible tells us that you love us so much. You died to save us, so please help us to live for you and always follow you.

Amen.

25. HOW CAN I GET RID OF MY SINS?

Lord Jesus,
help me to think about you, learn
more about you, and love you today.

READ: PSALM 51:1-12

How many sinful things do you think you have done in your life? A lot. You couldn't count them, could you? What can you do about all those sins? Can you put them in a trash bag and get rid of them? Of course not. So, is there any way we can get rid of our sins?

There is one way.

Sometimes our sins harm other people. King David harmed other people by his sins. But in Psalm 51:4 he wrote, 'Against You, You only have I sinned and done this evil in Your sight.' He harmed other people, but his sin was against God. That is always true.

But if my sin is against God, only God can forgive me. Only God can save me! So what can we do?

There is good news! The Bible tells us in John 3:16, 'For God so loved the world that He gave His only begotten Son, that whoever believes in Him should not perish but have everlasting life.'

What did Jesus do so that we could be forgiven?

Peter gives us the answer in 1 Peter 2:24: Jesus 'bore our sins in His own body on the tree.'

The tree Peter was writing about was the cross on which Jesus died for us. Can you picture what Jesus did? It is as if God were able to put all our sins in a huge trash bag and Jesus carried them on his shoulders onto the cross.

Imagine that bag, filled with all of your sins, being emptied all over Jesus when he was nailed to the cross. When he died for us, he carried them all away.

We can't get rid of our sins. But Jesus could. And he did. That is the wonderful message of the gospel!

No wonder we want to say 'thank you' to the Lord Jesus! Thank you, Jesus!

Lord Jesus,

Thank you that you took all our sins to the cross of Calvary! Help us not to be afraid of telling you that we have sinned. You would not have died for us unless you loved us. Thank you for wanting to forgive us. You are a wonderful Saviour. We love you.

Amen.

26. WILL JESUS EVER DIE AGAIN?

Lord Jesus,
help me to think about you, learn
more about you, and love you today.

READ: ROMANS 8:31-39

Do you remember what happened on the first Easter Sunday? Yes, Jesus rose from the dead.

But is it possible that Jesus might die again? What would happen to us then? No! Jesus will never die again. In Paul's Letter to the Romans, he says, 'We know that Christ, having been raised from the dead, dies no more' (Romans 6:9).

But why will Jesus never die again? Here are two important reasons:

First, God's Word tells us that when Jesus rose again he had the same body. But God the Father did something wonderful to change it so that it can never die. Nobody can kill Jesus again. He is alive for ever now.

There's a second reason that Jesus will never die again. He doesn't need to die again. He needed to die the first time for our sake. Only if he died in our place could our sins be forgiven. Because of that, all those who trust in Jesus as their Saviour will be with him in heaven. Then when he makes everything new, we will enjoy being with him in the new heavens and new earth. He doesn't need to die again. He has done everything that was needed to have our sins forgiven.

But how can I have my sins forgiven? By telling Jesus about them, and that you are sorry for them all. And then by asking the Lord Jesus to be your Saviour, and telling him you want him to be your Lord. You can pray like this: 'Lord Jesus you died on the cross for my sins. I am sorry for them, please forgive me. I am trusting you; please make me more like you. Amen.'

Jesus once said to a man he healed, 'Son, be of good cheer; your sins are forgiven you' (Matthew 9:2). It must have been wonderful to hear those words from Jesus' lips. But now Jesus says the same thing to us through his written word in the Bible.

Here are two things we can be sure about: Jesus will never die again; and those who trust him will always be with him.

Lord Jesus,

Thank you for dying on the cross for our sins. Thank you, Heavenly Father, for raising our Saviour from the dead. Thank you, Holy Spirit for working in our hearts to help us to see that Jesus is the Saviour we need.

Amen.

27. DO YOU NEED AN ADVOCATE?

Lord Jesus,
help me to think about you, learn
more about you, and love you today.

READ: 1 JOHN 14:15-18 AND 25-27

Do you know what an advocate does? An advocate is a kind of lawyer.

The word 'advocate' comes from two Latin words which mean 'towards' and 'to call'. So, an advocate is someone you call to help you. If you were accused of breaking the law, then you would need an advocate to speak up for you and defend you in a law court.

When we break God's law we need an advocate too. But we have a problem, don't we? We are guilty! We could never say to God, 'I didn't really sin' or 'It wasn't too bad, just let me off.' No, the Bible tells us we have all sinned and we deserve to be sent away from God's presence and blessing for ever. Is there an advocate who can speak up for us and help us?

Yes, there is! In 1 John 2:1-2 the apostle says: 'If anyone sins, we have an Advocate with the Father, Jesus Christ the righteous. And He Himself is the propitiation for our sins.'

What does that mean? It means that Jesus can help us even although we have sinned. He is the only one who can say, 'Dear Father, this person I represent pleads "guilty". But I have already taken the punishment they deserve (*that's what the big word 'propitiation' means*). I am asking you to accept what I have done in their place.' And our Heavenly Father accepts what Jesus has done for us as though we had done it ourselves!

Long before we go to Jesus to ask him to be our advocate, his Heavenly Father said to him, 'My dear Son, I love these people so much; but they are guilty. They need an advocate who will speak up for them. But they also need one who will take their punishment. Will you be that kind of advocate for them?' Long before he was born in Bethlehem, our Saviour said 'Yes, Father, I will be that kind of advocate for them.'

So, whenever you sin, don't hide from him. Go to him and say, 'Jesus, you have died for me. Will you be my advocate with the Father?' Jesus will say, 'Yes'. He promised he would!

Lord Jesus,

You know we have failed your Father. We are guilty of sin. Thank you for being our advocate and being willing to take our punishment. You love us very much; and we love you too. Thank you for being such a wonderful Saviour.

Amen.

Lord Jesus,
help me to think about you, learn
more about you, and love you today.

READ: PSALM 23:1-6

Do you ever lose things? Jesus once told a three-part story about things that were lost. The first part was about a shepherd who had a hundred sheep and one of them got lost. The second part was about a woman who had ten coins and lost one of them. The third part was about a father who had two sons. One of them ran away from home, and so he too was lost. You can read this three-part story in Luke chapter 15.

But let's concentrate on the first part just now. The shepherd lost one sheep out of a hundred. He might have thought, 'It's only one out of a hundred. I still have ninety-nine. It's no great loss. I'm not going to risk my life tonight trying to find a stupid sheep! I'll just stay at home.'

But Jesus said that when the shepherd discovered one of his sheep was missing he put all the other sheep in a safe field and set out to find it.

Do you think when he found it, he took out his rod and whacked the sheep all the way home? No. He picked it up and carried it home. That sheep probably weighed one hundred pounds!

The Bible tells us that we are like lost sheep. We have wandered away from God. We can't find our own way back. But Jesus is our Good Shepherd. He came from heaven and made the dangerous journey to find us and save us.

Jesus said that the shepherd found his sheep and brought it home on his shoulders 'rejoicing'.

Jesus is like that shepherd. We mustn't ever be afraid to tell him we need him to save us.

There is a famous hymn about this story. It is called 'There were ninety and nine'. One of its verses says:

> *None of the ransomed ever knew,*
> *how deep were the waters crossed,*
> *Or how dark was the night that the Lord past through,*
> *before finding the sheep that was lost.*

We'll never know how much Jesus loved us. But we can thank him and tell him we love him.

Lord Jesus,

Thank you for all you suffered in order to save us from our sins. And thank you that instead of being critical of us, and complaining about us, you love us and are happy when we trust you as our Saviour and Lord. Help us to do that today.

Amen.

29. CAN WHAT TASTES BAD DO GOOD?

Lord Jesus,
help me to think about you, learn
more about you, and love you today.

READ: PROVERBS 3:1-12

Do you like broccoli? It is supposed to be good for you. But some people don't like its taste! It's funny, isn't it, that we don't always like the things that are good for us!

One day I went to get some medicine. I saw a sign that said if I paid a little extra for my medicine, they would add something to it to make it taste better! I thought, 'That's strange. Why can't they just make it taste better to begin with?'

The medicine I got when I was young usually tasted horrible. But my mum often said, 'Take it. It doesn't taste good because it is doing you good!'

There are lots of things that we don't much like at the time, that are good for us. Some of us don't like hard work, or doing sums, or learning to spell, or gym times at school. But they are all good for us. Sometimes we find that out later.

However, that is not our only problem. There are also things that we like that aren't good for us. Is there a simple way we can learn to tell the difference? Yes. Here it is:

Everything Jesus likes is good for us.
Everything Jesus doesn't like is bad for us.

Sometimes the devil comes along and whispers, 'Jesus wants to give you things that you won't enjoy. So what he wants must be bad for you.' Or he'll say, 'Jesus doesn't want you to do this, but I'm telling you that you'll enjoy it.'

Whose voice will you listen to? Which voice can you trust?

You can trust what Jesus says in his word the Bible. You can be sure that everything Jesus wants to do in your life is for your good. And you can trust him when he says that the devil is a liar.

But how can we be sure that Jesus wants only what is best for us? Because he was willing to die for us on the cross. If he did that for you, don't you think you can trust him?

Lord Jesus,

You always want to do us good! We know things happen in our lives that we don't like and find difficult. But we thank you that you want what is best for us. We know you died for us, and we know the devil didn't. Please help us always to choose what pleases you.

Amen.

Lord Jesus,
help me to think about you, learn
more about you, and love you today.

READ: 1 CORINTHIANS 15:50-57

Did anything make Jesus sad? Yes. Do you know the shortest verse in the Bible? It's John's Gospel 11:35. It has only two words: 'Jesus wept'.

One of Jesus' best friends, called Lazarus, had died. Lazarus's sisters, Mary and Martha were upset. Jesus was very sad. He went to comfort them.

When my mother died, there was a funeral service. At the end, just as we were about to leave the service, I saw a single tear was running down the cheek of one of my young children. I remembered how tears ran down Jesus' face once. I thought, 'It's alright, Jesus understands. You can tell Jesus all about this.'

Jesus does understand. He has been sad too.

Jesus brought Lazarus back to life again. You can read the story of how he did that in John's Gospel chapter 11. He showed that he was able to take away sadness.

Jesus has promised that one day he will take away all sadness. There will be no more pain, or tears. And there will be no more death. Everyone who has trusted in Jesus will be with him and with one another for ever and ever! We should think about that when we are sad. When will that happen? It will happen when the Lord Jesus returns. He will bring all of us in his family together again.

That hasn't happened yet, has it? There are still things that make us sad. But until he comes back again, we can remember the shortest verse in the Bible, 'Jesus wept.' It will remind us that he understands. He is still the same Jesus who stood at the grave of Lazarus and wept. He still understands when we are sad. And we can still go to him, and ask him to help us, to stay with us, and to be our Saviour and Friend.

He will. Have you asked him yet?

Lord Jesus,

We thank you that you have been sad, and you understand what it's like. Please be with our friends who are sad, or sore, or lonely today. Thank you that you have the power to make the sad become glad. Help us always to trust you and love you.

Amen.

31. HOW CAN I BE SURE JESUS LOVES ME?

*Lord Jesus,
help me to think about you, learn
more about you, and love you today.*

READ: MARK 14:12-26

Do you know the song, 'Jesus loves me, this I know'?
How do we know he loves us? The next line of the song
tells us: 'For the Bible tells me so.'

There are three ways we show that we love somebody,
aren't there? We tell them we love them; we do things
for them because we love them; and we give them gifts
that say, 'I love you'. Jesus also shows his love for us in
these three ways.

Way number one: He tells us often in the Bible how
much he loves us.

Way number two: Jesus has also done something for
us to show how much he loves us. You know what that
is, don't you? He didn't need to come into our world at

all. But he came into it and lived in it and died on the cross for our sins—all because he loved us so much.

Way number three: Jesus wanted to give us all a gift that would tell us how much he loved us.

I wonder if you can guess what that gift is. You have probably seen it. But you may have to think hard to get the answer: it is the Lord's Supper. We also call it 'the Communion service' because Jesus has promised to be with us.

The Lord's Supper is the part of the church service where we are given a piece of bread to eat and some wine to drink, just as Jesus told the disciples to do. It's as if Jesus himself were giving us the bread and the wine and saying, 'I am with you. So, eat this broken bread and drink this wine, and remember that I died for you because I love you so much.' And just as we take the bread and the wine into ourselves, we take the Lord Jesus into our hearts.

As we do that, we remember what Paul said in Galatians 2:20. Jesus is 'the Son of God, who loved me, and gave Himself for me.' Can you say that too?

We have reached the last chapter of this book. If you have never said that before, why don't you speak to the Lord Jesus about it now?

Lord Jesus,

At the end of this book we want to tell you that we know we have sinned. We need you to be our Saviour. So please help us to trust in you and to turn our backs on sin. Thank you for dying on the cross for us, and rising again, and promising to be with us for ever.

Amen.

Conclusion

Well, you have made it right to the end of the book! Well done! I hope you have enjoyed it and that it has helped you to think about the Lord Jesus, to trust him, and to love him more.

Most of the books I have written are for grown-ups. So why does someone who writes for grown-ups want to write books for children as well? There are lots of reasons, but since we're at the end of the book now, maybe I should mention only two.

The first is that when the Lord Jesus was on earth he loved children, and children loved him. And that's still true! He wants you to know that, and he wants you to trust him as your Saviour and love him as your Lord. Books about him can help us to do that. I hope this one has helped you.

The second reason is this. Although I am a grown-up, I was once one of the children who needed to learn about Jesus' love for me. And so, when I was your age, I started reading the Bible each day, and asking the Lord to help me to understand it. I hope you will do the same. The Bible is a big book—actually there are 66 books in it—and I needed help to read it and understand it. Two books you might find helpful are *66 Books One Story* and *Read With Me*.[1]

---

1. Paul Reynolds, *66 Books One Story*, (Christian Focus Publications, Tain, Ross-shire, Scotland, 2013) ISBN: 978-1-84550-819-7.
Jean Stapleton, *Read With Me*, (Christian Focus Publications, Tain, Ross-shire, Scotland, 2006) ISBN: 978-1-84550-148-8.

So I hope you will start reading the Bible when you are young. But try not to make the mistake I did! I thought that reading the Bible each day was the same thing as being a Christian. It was a while before I realised that although that's important, it's not the same as knowing and trusting the Lord Jesus himself. Then, one day, I was reading the words of Jesus in John's Gospel chapter 5 verses 39-40. He said to some people who were listening to him: 'You search the Scriptures, for in them you think you have eternal life; and these are they which testify of Me. But you are not willing to come to Me that you may have life.' I realised that Jesus was not just speaking to people long ago who made that mistake. I had made it too. He was speaking to me!

I knew then that I must pray that he would help me to come to him, to trust him, and to get to know him. Some time later, Jesus' words in John's Gospel chapter 8, verse 12 helped me to do that: 'Then Jesus spoke to them again, saying, "I am the light of the world. He who follows Me shall not walk in darkness, but have the light of life."' He has kept his promise!

So now you know why I wanted to write this book! And now I hope you will want to read the very best book—the Bible—yourself. Maybe you could start by reading John's Gospel.

May you know the love and presence of the Lord Jesus every day!

Sinclair B. Ferguson

In this devotional book for children, Sinclair Ferguson helps our children to know what Jesus has done for them. He traces the life of Jesus from womb to tomb, from cradle to throne. By the end, every child will know what it really means to sing, "Jesus loves me this I know, for the Bible tells me so." A great source for children, parents, and pastors!

Jonny Gibson
Associate Professor of Old Testament,
Westminster Theological Seminary;
Author of *The Moon Is Always Round*

Good news is hard to come by these days. This book by my friend Dr. Ferguson is a welcome help. He helps us discover the best Book that tells us the best news about who God is and what He has done for His people. It's a true story that begins before time began, and it's a glorious story we will be telling one another for eternity. May your love for God grow as you enter into this story. I hope we can talk about it together some day.

Chris Larson
President & CEO
Ligonier Ministries

TRUTH FOR LIFE®

THE BIBLE-TEACHING MINISTRY OF **ALISTAIR BEGG**

The mission of Truth For Life is to teach the Bible with clarity and relevance so that unbelievers will be converted, believers will be established, and local churches will be strengthened.

Daily Program

Each day, Truth For Life distributes the Bible teaching of Alistair Begg across the U.S. and in several locations outside of the U.S. through 2,000 radio outlets. To find a radio station near you, visit **truthforlife.org/stationfinder**.

Free Teaching

The daily program, and Truth For Life's entire teaching library of over 3,000 Bible-teaching messages, can be accessed for free online at **truthforlife.org** and through Truth For Life's mobile app, which can be download for free from your app store.

At-Cost Resources

Books and audio studies from Alistair Begg are available for purchase at cost, with no markup. Visit **truthforlife.org/store**.

Where to Begin?

If you're new to Truth For Life and would like to know where to begin listening and learning, find starting point suggestions at **truthforlife.org/firststep**. For a full list of ways to connect with Truth For Life, visit **truthforlife.org/subscribe**.

Contact Truth For Life

P.O. Box 398000 Cleveland, Ohio 44139
phone 1 (888) 588-7884   **email** letters@truthforlife.org
truthforlife.org

CHRISTIAN FOCUS PUBLICATIONS

Christian Focus | Christian Heritage | CF4K | Mentor

Christian Focus Publications publishes books for adults and children under its four main imprints: Christian Focus, CF4K, Mentor and Christian Heritage. Our books reflect our conviction that God's Word is reliable and Jesus is the way to know him, and live for ever with him.

Our children's publication list covers pre-school to early teens. We also publish personal and family devotional titles, biographies and inspirational stories that children will love.

From pre-school board books to teenage apologetics, we have it covered!

Christian Focus Publications Ltd,
Geanies House, Fearn, Ross-shire,
IV20 1TW, Scotland,
United Kingdom.
www.christianfocus.com

CF4•K
Because you're never
too young to know Jesus